THE LION AND THE MOUSE

NARRATED BY THE TIMID BUT TRUTHFUL MOUSE

BY NANCY LOEWEN

ILLUSTRATED BY CRISTIAN BERNARDINI

PICTURE WINDOW BOOKS
a capstone imprint

Editor: Jill Kalz
Designer: Lori Bye
Premedia Specialist: Kris Wilfahrt
The illustrations in this book were created digitally.
Design Element: Shutterstock, Andrey_Kuzman

Picture Window Books
1710 Roe Crest Drive
North Mankato, MN 56003
www.mycapstone.com

Copyright © 2019 by Picture Window Books, a Capstone imprint. All rights reserved. No part of this publication may be reproduced in whole or in part, or stored in a retrieval system, or transmitted in any form or by any means, electronic, mechanical, photocopying, recording, or otherwise, without written permission of the publisher.

Library of Congress Cataloging-in-Publication Data
Names: Loewen, Nancy, 1964– author. | Bernardini, Cristian, 1975– illustrator.
Title: The lion and the mouse, narrated by the timid but truthful mouse / by Nancy Loewen ; illustrated by Cristian Bernardini.
Description: North Mankato, Minnesota : Picture Window Books, [2018] | Series: Nonfiction picture books. The other side of the fable |
Summary: In this humorous retelling of the classic fable told by a mouse, Catnip is the bold mouse who is caught by the lion (she really should not have tried to jump over him)—but it is her timid twin sister, Bitsy, who finds the courage to fulfill her sister's promise, and chews through the net the lion gets caught in.
Identifiers: LCCN 2018005706 (print) | LCCN 2018006555 (ebook) | ISBN 9781515828747 (eBook PDF) | ISBN 9781515828662 (library binding) | ISBN 9781515828709 (paperback)
Subjects: LCSH: Fables. | Mice—Juvenile fiction. | Lion—Juvenile fiction. | Twins—Juvenile fiction. | Promises—Juvenile fiction. | Humorous stories. | CYAC: Fables. | Mice—Fiction. | Lion—Fiction. | Twins—Fiction. | Sisters—Fiction. | Promises—Fiction. | Humorous stories. | LCGFT: Fables. | Humorous fiction.
Classification: LCC PZ8.2.L63 (ebook) | LCC PZ8.2.L63 Li 2018 (print) | DDC [E]—dc23
LC record available at https://lccn.loc.gov/2018005706

Printed in the United States.
PA021

A fable is a short animal tale that teaches a lesson. It is one of the oldest story forms. "The Lion and the Mouse" is from a collection of hundreds of fables called *Aesop's Fables*. These stories may have been written by Aesop, a Greek storyteller who lived from 620 to 560 BC.

A lion was sleeping in the forest when a mouse scampered across his nose. The lion was very angry about being woken up. He lifted his huge paw to kill the mouse.

"Let me go!" begged the mouse. "I promise I'll repay you someday."

The lion laughed. "You? How could a little thing like you ever help me?"

But he let the mouse go.

A few days later, the lion became caught in a hunter's net. The mouse recognized the lion's roars and ran to help. She chewed at the ropes until the lion was free.

"You see? I told you I'd repay you!" the mouse said. "Even a tiny mouse can help a lion."

The moral of the story:
One act of kindness deserves another.

Hello! I'm Bitsy. That fable you just read? It's missing some key details. I know because I was there.

Tell me, do you have any brothers or sisters? Do you ever feel invisible—like they don't even see you?

Do you ever wish you could do something to get their attention?

Well, *that's* what this fable is *really* about.

I have a twin sister, Catnip. We look alike, but that's about all we have in common.

Catnip is great at sports. She won the Tail-ball Championship and the Treetop Challenge. She even won third place in the Owl Bowl! She and her friends run around the forest, jumping off the highest vines and chasing the scariest shadows.

Me? I barely got through Puddle Paddling class. My hobbies are weaving baskets and hunting for letter-shaped sticks.

Until the lion came along, Catnip never asked me to play with her. But the lion changed all that.

One day while I was braiding my whiskers, I overheard Catnip and her friends. They were talking about their next adventure.

". . . and we'll climb over the log and run around the prickle shrub three times. Then we'll touch the golden flower, hop over the sleeping lion, and climb to the top of the bitternut tree!"

I shuddered just thinking about it. Especially the part about the lion. That didn't seem very smart to me. A race was one thing, but *lion hopping?*

A few minutes later, I heard an awful sound.

ROAR!

The lion was awake!

I was terrified, but I ran to see if Catnip needed help.

Snarling and showing his teeth, the lion held his huge paw over Catnip. Would this be the end of my twin sister?

"Let me go!" Catnip begged. "If you spare my life, maybe someday I will save yours!"

The lion twitched his tail a few times. Then he began to laugh. "You? Save me?" he said. "Why, you're no bigger than a leaf!"

"I might be small, but there's a lot I can do," Catnip said.

The lion lifted his paw. "Go," he said. "You woke me up from my nap, but at least you made me laugh."

Catnip darted toward us. We all caught our breath.

That was close!

For a few days, Catnip stayed near home. She was actually nice to me. We painted our nails. We went on pebble hunts together.

But soon Catnip went back to her friends. And I was invisible again.

One afternoon, I was watching Catnip and her pals do high dives from Riddle Rock. All of a sudden, we heard—

ROAR! ROAR! RRROOOOAAAAARRRRR!

The lion was in trouble!

I ran out to Catnip. "Come on!" I shouted. "Maybe the lion needs you!"

We found the lion tangled up in a hunter's net.

"Go, chew through those ropes," I said, nudging Catnip. "Set him free before the hunter comes back!"

Catnip froze. "I can't do that," she said, her eyes wide.

"But you promised you would repay the lion for sparing your life!" I said.

"Yes, but I didn't think I'd really have to do it!" she said.

RRROOOOAAAAARRRRR!

I knew the lion would be in great danger if someone didn't help him.

Then I thought, what if *I* helped? This was my big chance. If *I* freed the lion, I would be doing something very kind and very, very brave. And I would never be invisible again!

I ran out to the lion before I could change my mind. "It's me!" I said, trying to make my voice sound like Catnip's. "If you stay still, I will chew through these ropes."

The lion stared at me. "Do you mean it?" he asked.

I nodded.

He calmed down, and I got to work. I chewed. And chewed. And chewed.

One by one, the ropes snapped.

Finally the lion was able to twist himself free.

"I'm sorry I laughed at you," he said. "You were right—a mouse *can* help a lion!" Then he bounded off into the forest.

I turned around. Catnip and her friends were watching me with their mouths hanging open.

"Wow, Sis," Catnip said. "You were amazing."

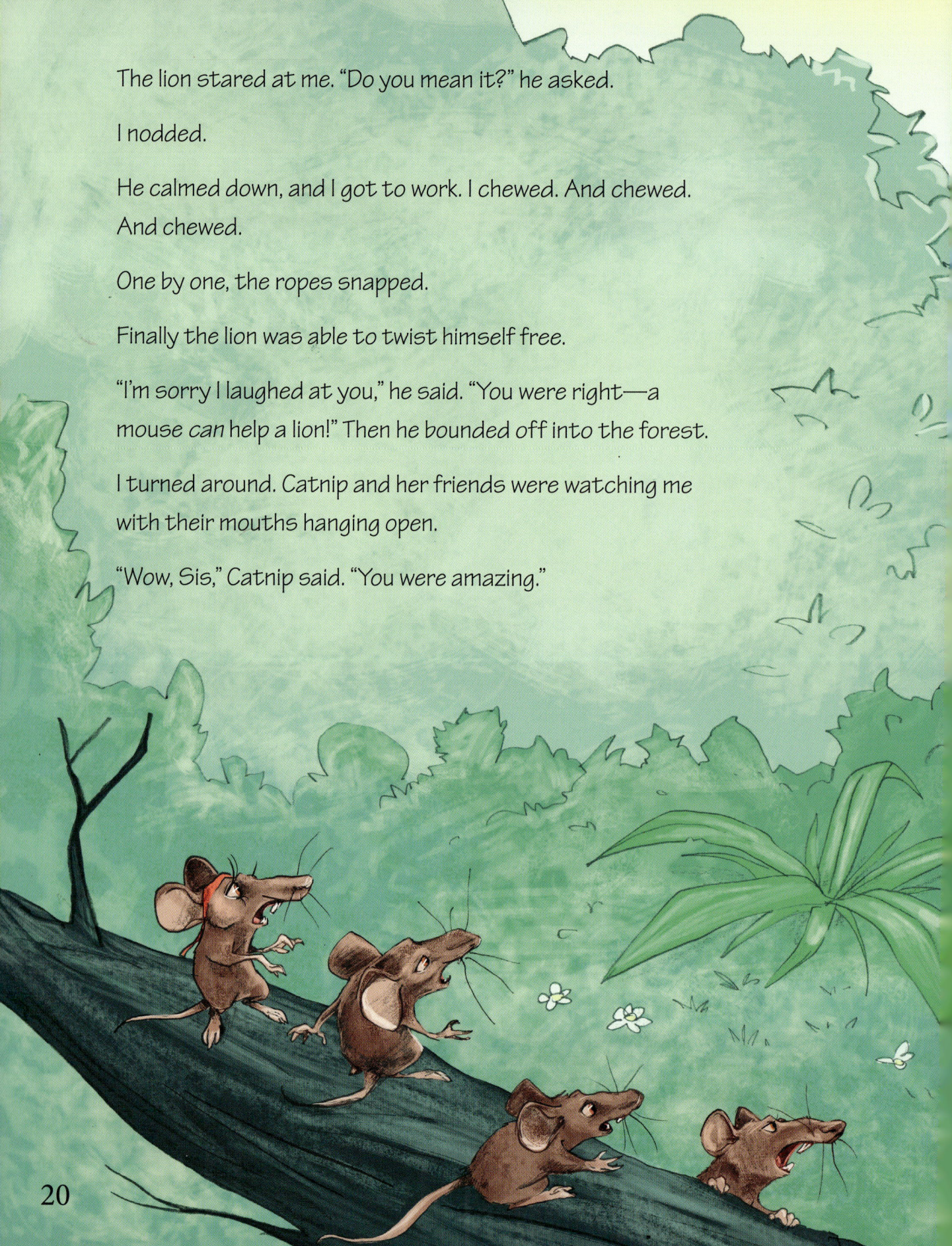

Since then, Catnip has played with me every day. I'm getting a lot better at kick-the-acorn. And it turns out that Catnip is very good at spotting letter-shaped sticks.

So what's the moral of *this* story?

Those who show great kindness (and bravery) can never be invisible. And that's the truth.

THINK ABOUT IT

Describe at least three ways in which Bitsy's version of the fable is different from the original fable.

If this story were told from Catnip's point of view, how might it change?

Do you think Catnip's character should have been the one to save the lion? Why or why not?

What do you think is more important: to be kind or to be brave? Explain your answer.

GLOSSARY

Aesop (AY-sop)—a Greek storyteller (620–560 BC) whose fables teach a lesson

character—a person, animal, or creature in a story

fable—a short animal tale that teaches a lesson

invisible—not seen

moral—a lesson about what is right and wrong

point of view—a way of looking at something

snarl—to growl with bared teeth

version—an account of something from a certain point of view

READ MORE

Broom, Jenny. *The Lion and the Mouse.* Somerville, Mass.: Templar Books, 2014.

Hoena, Blake, retold by. *The Lion and the Mouse.* Classic Fables in Rhythm and Rhyme. North Mankato, Minn.: Cantata Learning, 2018.

Olmstead, Kathleen, told by. *The Lion and the Mouse.* Silver Penny Stories. New York: Sterling Children's Books, 2014.

INTERNET SITES

Use FactHound to find Internet sites related to this book.

Visit *www.facthound.com*

Just type in 9781515828662 and go.

LOOK FOR ALL THE BOOKS IN THE SERIES:

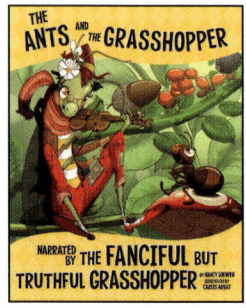 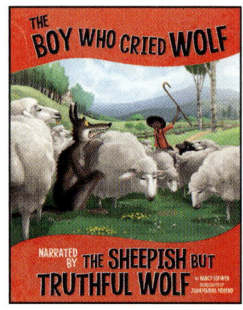  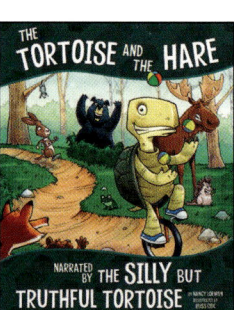